The ACOLYTE

The ACOLYTE

Poems by
NANCY HIGHTOWER

Port Yonder Press

Shellsburg, Iowa

Port Yonder Press
6332 33rd Avenue Drive
Shellsburg, Iowa 52332
www.portyonderpress.com

ISBN 9781935600497

Book cover design by Francesca Myman

Book cover art by Anna O'Brien

Editor: Chila Woychik

Consulting Editor: Francesca Myman

First paperback edition, 2015

Printed in the U.S.A.

CONTENTS

REM

I am forever making an entrance,
bumping into empty spaces:
vacant lodge, the room with one bed,
the darkened waterpark, and the house
where I killed.
My heart beats sideways, paper doll, paper thin,
as I suction myself across
the creamy landscape, reading locations.
Inside the room—a bed
suspended mid-air,
a spiral staircase springs up to meet it,
and the little girl
is sometimes there,
tries to remember my name,
sees me slithering across the board
on my way out.
In between the rafters of waking,
I split myself into a pair of eyes,
      bulging, waiting.

PTL: CIRCA 1981

In the murky chalet
burnt orange carpet crawls under my feet,
flushes out the flavor of sienna walls,
makes everything look like
hell had decorated it.
Everyone crashes
into dim lighting,
early bedtimes.

Somewhere in a corner
curled up, a little girl watches,
hands folded.   Prays
for her eyes to be opened
with fire and brimstone.
In stark revelation, hears
whispers grunting salvation,
muffled shouts of oh Christ,
and the slow moan of redemption
finally crashing down.

In the south
things happen.
My mother's belly juts out malignantly;
Jim says it's God's doing.
My father,   standing in awe,   speaks in tongues;
I see them now
through the light of dirty water
as if the very color of that place
drove them all crazy.

INSOMNIA

Manic sunsets lie in your eyes,
twisted hues of pink and cream.
Tonight we sleep,
dreams to thicken against the eye's wall.
Tongues thrown down,
clamped into grinding teeth,
a blood-letting of milk and honey.
Your hair is wet by midnight,
plastered down by dawn.
We are full to the brim
with nightfall.

DROUGHT

There is comfort in winter, snow-peaked
crescent moons, the cold bitten skin
on hands, an icing over of bad summers.
We expect a certain consistency regarding seasons,
a dying when the time is right, the pleasant aspect
of going numb, sleet and madness.

But this winter is different, warmer.
No freezing rain pelts my face or forces
my head down in submission,
no wind to drive the body
back under heavy quilt where
I shed all my scales, smooth myself
back into the shell.

Instead, a strange sun bullies
across the sky, blinds me with its insolence.
I hurl sweaters aside, leaving
their comforted bulk and thick weave
for a flimsy shirt, arms bare and the elbows
dark and patched. I am misplaced,
standing under the wrong day,
and the night is far worse, a nocturnal desert
which sweats me out by three a.m.
My dreams, though, are spiked with icicles,
dirty-white and hanging like daggers above the bed.
Each morning I wake,
my eyes pierced with water.

SOME OTHER STORY

In the belly it hides,
a gutted ship
rising up, resting
at the base of your throat,
broken words ready
to be purged.

Your body
knows something
is to be missed:
pictures that run through
displaced lands, strange cities
uttering forgotten visions.
Like a prophet, it travels
through you in sheepskin,
wanting baptism.

But on certain days
it will visit again,
an old man with hands outstretched,
blessing your eyes, feeding you
berries from the sun.

My Mother's Madness

The memory returns
every January, blurred
like rain on a cracked window.
The ground around us shifting
as narratives were bent and tilted,
Hades ascending.

You left with him
just before the witching hour,
silty loam and mud freezing solid for the winter.
I summoned Lazarus
for his official position on the matter,
gummed pomegranate seeds
and asked Orpheus for the handbook
on calling back lost ones.
This was no abduction, they cried,
no death but your own.

Nonetheless, every year
my hands grow numb, turn into
clumsy birds fluttering against
our burial, a frantic clawing
of fingers raked in dirt,
stained beyond recognition.
By dusk I curl up, rooted to the spot,
and wait for summer,
for a torrent of suns to unleash
and wash me clean.

RITUAL

The pebble sits heavy
in my hand, palm moistened
from the curled fist
cradling its smooth outline.
When fingers open,
it turns black to sight
even though its true color
is ultramarine; still, it sits
like sin among my lifelines,
tries to roll back over
the grave of Christ.

The voice draped in candlelight
tells me to speak my burdens
into the dark round glass,
and then place it, like a cast-off coffin,
on the table, where my fear
will grow cold and forgotten.

I want to throw the stone
onto the floor, splintering
all my sorrows—
scratched arms and blacked out nights,
the bartender and priest who both
know me by name, thoughts dark and hard
and always beyond the reach of God.

So I keep my token, hold it up
between two fingers against the dim

ray of candle and catch for a split moment
the shudder of blue violet exposed,
defiant to its own opaque existence—
see a beauty stained forever
with the ache for light.

CREATION

The turbulent wait
as   breath   erupts   in
ecstatic gasps.
I dream of you
draped in aurora borealis,
stars swathed around your belly.
The sky hardens, cracks into
Pleiades   Orion   Andromeda.

My fingers stroke your throat;
still your voice is silent, dust-dry.
The sunset melts into amber,
trapping me in the thrum
of the sparrow's heart.

My hands keep working the clay.
I see your eyes beginning,
the rise and fall of your chest.
When will you finally look
into my face and live?

EVE

Your last glance melted
into branches as I wiped
the juice off your mouth.

Now we're muted in ivy,
my stomach, stretched and empty.
Your back glistens with sweat.
At night, I become a blind puzzle,
voluptuously divided—
        lips   breast   thigh
a weight to be laid down and tasted.

In this only, death seems welcome—
that you may once again look upon me
with eyes uncursed.

ABEL

Under my shadow you dabbled in the clay,
making a garden of delights out of mud pies.
We were sons of earth until that hour
when the ram's fat smoked like Christ.
Then I knew you to be the angel,
sweet boy, knew you would fly
into heaven while I clawed
my way through dust and snakes.

When we cobbled our way
through the field that late afternoon,
I drank visions of molten fruit,
wanted to see redemption in the dying red
of your smile, and so I struck forward,
eyes closed, straight to the place
where hair swept across brow.

As your head sunk down
into a bright puddle, you called
out my name only once,
but the word bore itself
straight through my chest,
a scar which marked forever
the loss of everything.

FLOOD

I didn't know then
that when the voice said *build*,
it meant no empire, no manor, no palace of delight
where we could feed ourselves
from tended gardens, no castle to keep
us from hearing the squalor of streets, or prison
to hold growing brutality at bay.

Rather, there was nervous packing,
a thunderous shuffling of hooves
and skirts bundling down into
deep rooms, sunless corners.

Enclosed in wood and animal dung,
we heard the rain start with drizzled frenzy
until the deep lifted itself up and rolled back
to the beginning, a formless place
of dark waters, angry spirits.

For months we floated
through the world's graveyard
and dreamt of stillness in the heart
while the dove grew weary of her flights.
When at last our feet sunk into muddy ground,
we gave thanks, as survivors often do.

I had deemed that the end to the story,
wanted to close my sight to a blank land,
        exiled years.

But the sky called me back with confusing light,
passionate shards breaking through into fractal arc,
and I saw a beauty that would someday pierce
hands and feet with bloodstained ravage.

I thought it, at the time, a dangerous promise,
to never again shed tears such as this—
to love a world you'd die for.

TAMAR

Tell me how many men
must I have roll off me
in the night and wake
to find my husbands dead again?
Black widowed into whoredom,
I am a patient woman, waiting
lifetimes, sitting on the side of the road,
ready to grasp with both hands
a lonely soul needing night-comfort.

There is a journey
through the realm of curses,
barrenness to push
in front of you—a broken cart,
God's displeasure,
call it what you will.

Still, I plan to take the lion by the mane
and wrestle him till dawn,
wear his bracelet
and pretty trinkets
until twins claw their way
into history, scarlet-bound.

Every step
a bruise closer
to the serpent's head.

SARAH

They prophesy over me, saying
when are you two getting pregnant?
How long have you been trying?
My womb, a chrysalis where
I might morph into an actual *woman*,
breasts that drip milk into a king's mouth.

Yet nothing stirs inside this belly,
no nausea to wake me
every morning into hope.
I told him today
go to her and make me a child,
choking on rosebushes
as the words left my mouth,
my teeth, thorns.

Now I lie here alone, my arms
shriveling into branches, fingering a dusty pool
of memories. When night falls I am locked
into sleep, a dark storm of swaddled bodies,
sweated tongues, lips bit into kisses.
There, in the turning, her moans
thunder across my heart, flashing me whispers
of the famined life to come.

SARAH (REVISITED)

There's no surviving the death of a child.
I have been many things: sister, wife, lover,
the woman who laughed at God,
and wanted fertility treatments.

But never this madness, this sacrifice.
You were the gift of old Christmases,
a memory to be born, my promised starlight.
The first time I gave you up almost killed me
as you left the cradle of my body, now pruned with age.

The second time, I didn't expect to outlive the day,
heard your coffin clap down
on my heart when the commandment came,
resounding into womb, into wailing wall.
For three days my eyes traveled towards the mountains,
praying for a change in the wind,
a breaking of God's heart.
When the hills finally smoked,
sent up the sweet savor of scorched flesh,
I fell into my grave with dry sobbing sounds.
Tears would not come—
how can one ask again
for a river in the desert?

Doppelganger (Leah)

I wore her favorite dress, the one
you accidentally stained with wine the night
you met our parents and babbled
about love at first sight. You wanted
to believe my body was hers, called me
by her name over and over again
once the dress was off, and I held on
believing that perhaps by morning
your words would come true.

JACOB'S TALE

One's life can be read through bodies:

My arms reach out to steal my brother's blessing,
then, legs twist around my waist
and in the darkness I press my lips
against a salty neck, crying out her name
home   home   home.
Yet when morning comes
I see only a stranger.

Seven years I live a slave for love,
leaving with two wives instead of one and
warring sons who throw themselves
into starlight, limbs askew,
burning out their stories one by one.
Later, they tell me my dearest boy is dead,
torn apart by some wild, sand-whipped thing.
They give me his coat to smell, colors muted,
my eyes finally blinded.
I believe the scent, just like my father did.

How many deserts does it take to come full circle?
In that muddy darkness, I wrestled God,
felt his body break under my own grief,
hip unhinged, our journey hobbled.

In the gap of dried blood, shrunk muscle,
a deceiver unmasks himself,
peels back the skull and bones and waits
to be reborn by the edge of a river.

PHARAOH

They eat brick and mortar
and beg for healthcare,
never ceasing to multiply,
like a bad math problem.

I tried reverse psychology,
killing the boys
instead of the girls,
but they hid the river rat
who would eventually sink his teeth
into my firstborn. Scavengers, all,
setting fire to the bushes
and crying *holy holy holy,*

I will gladly send you back to your god,
your Yahweh, this Jehovah, one by one
till you have subtracted yourselves,
becoming zero. Damn bastards,
I have had enough of your plagues.

MOSES
(Numbers 20:7-12)

The night is divided by locusts,
everyone gold-dusted and aching.
Seraphim waltzing,
doomed to wandering.

The camp dissolves into a murmur
of tangled limbs, haunted desire
for darkness unhemmed by cloud and fire.

My eyes remain locked on the rock face,
moon drenched enough
to show the bruise.
My   staff   fallen
as you continue to weep,
quenching the people's thirst.

I am no better than most.
Even Psyche lost the battle with doubt,
scarred her lover in a moment of impulse.
The epic quest begins with agony.
Taunted by sunrise, we battle
serpents   Cerberus and siblings
who cry out   why   not   us?

Hunting
for the whisper
of that faceless voice,

there being   time   enough
for promised lands, calmer seas.
Bread   from   heaven
this hunger
this breathtaking exile.

AARON

Plagues are such strange things
swimming through you, an unearthly,
multi-limbed creature with slow dances in its arms.

Take my two youngest boys,
my babies. One day they played
with strange fire; unlike what my brother saw
flaming within a bush, this blaze had no holiness
about it, and so God burnt them up,
like paper dolls. With their ashes
I daubed up my eyes and moved on.

That's the nature of plagues,
to arrive unbidden, a sad relative
who comes to die upon you, the air
soured by their breath.

There was the day we both saw it coming
with our tribes angry, driven to go back
to where there was meat and work,
a sacrifice to simple gods—earrings
and a sprinkle of blood.
Their cries spanned the desert floor,
rose up to heaven. Then we felt it,
the wind's changing, the sick smell,
saw everyone crumpling into
fetal position, arms flailing like newborns,
the bodies falling, slow and beautiful as the sea.

And I stood there in between the living and dead,
arms outspread: a broken symbol of atonement,
blessing all. My sons' faces wavered
before me like a mirage.
When I reached out to caress their cheeks
one last time, that's when
the rains came, God's weeping with
a father's rage at watching children turn and turn,
blowing away like dust.

JERICHO

The circle marches
slow every day,
voices mute within
the trumpeted hum,
dimming all silence.

But our death began
much earlier, with the sound of
sea closing in over Egypt,
unleashed terror upon chariots,
tearing horses into dog-meat.
It's the way of all holocausts,
to start with the animals.

The river gave less trouble,
and merely rolled back
into red carpet, plush like blood.
When the horns blew their sad music,
our gate shivered, was laid flat on its face
as an army trampled through,
a wild herd of claws and teeth.

Their swords slashed through
our children like lightning and the men,
(boys really), and women
were ripped into fragments, scraps
thrown into the old list:
  Auschwitz   Dachau   Warsaw

It's the way of cursed people—
to have their names unwritten,
the walls always falling.

*Then Jael, Heber's wife, took a nail of the tent, and took a hammer
in her hand, and went softly unto him, and smote the nail into his
temples, and fastened it to the ground: for he was fast asleep and
weary. So he died.*—Judges 4:21

JAEL

Such a muted sound at first
as spike hits skin, then,
the skull's soft crunch.
One would think murder made more noise—
like a battering ram against the temple,
but no, just a simple tent nail
and a cup of milk;
we women have our ways.

Had I more time, I would have cooked,
made the bed, washed the dishes—
scheduled in the killing.
But he had come quickly, galloped
himself into my sanctuary,
heaving breath in muffled gasps
and war-weary, as men often are.

I became an eagle, feathers spread,
talons reaching as I flew out to meet him,
and he, thinking I was his dove, his mother hen,
came under my wings, shadow-filled.
I wrapped their warmth around him with
my voice spinning lies, quilted comfort,
my hands tucking in the folds of the blanket

as he slipped into that dream-quenching slumber.
I almost kissed his brow
to drive the pin through.

His mother, far away,
felt the breeze of my hand as it came down,
gentle, a loving breath upon her cheek,
thought her son had come back early in victory,
and opened her arms wide in ready embrace.
When she turned,
her eyes beheld nothing
but leaves falling
in the wind.

SAMSON AND SOLOMON

Once, there were two men:
One was the strongest man in the world,
broke pillars like they were toothpicks,
made Hercules look like a toddler.
The other was as wise as a genie,
saw through people's wishes
for the broken-hearted tricksters they were.

Enticed by the pulse and hum of love,
each loved the tantalizing riddle,
honey tongued in the lion's mouth,
more golden than any temple.
Wrapped in its gaze,
they became blinded by the doe eyes
and coy-cocked head,
a smile so serene it could glide into
the mouth like butter, gilded sugar,
lips that coaxed the soul
to sleep upon any altar.

Kingdoms crumbled around them
as they clamored for one last kiss,
but could they, amidst the roar
of falling walls and the Sphinx's laughter,
hear the Spirit's sadness
as it whispered goodbye?

*And Jephthah made a vow to the LORD: "If you give the
Ammonites into my hands, whatever comes out of the door of my
house to meet me when I return in triumph from the Ammonites
will be the LORD's, and I will sacrifice it as a burnt
offering"...When Jephthah returned to his home in Mizpah, who
should come out to meet him but his daughter, dancing to the
sound of timbrels.*—Judges 11:30-34

JEPHTHAH

I was a slut's son, and burned my daughter.
Broken warrior that I am—fired-forged,
and meant to judge.
   No ram to appear
and save me from my oath,
only her eyes
   looking through me,
prophesying desolate years to come
with the advent of her loss.

Meanwhile, I live sword drawn,
remembering old treacheries.
Nations gather, and I am called
like a dog to the ring,
ready to fight the god of war,
all his children smoldering over
forgotten battle lines, old kinships.

We will win, of course,
like they do in all the good stories,
but tell me this:

As I begin my bewildering rule
over this wayward people,
and sit in the judgment chair

listening to all their broken promises,
who will avenge my loneliness
or cradle my little girl's ashes?

But the men would not listen to him. So the man took his concubine
and sent her outside to them, and they raped her and abused
her throughout the night, and at dawn they let her go. At daybreak
the woman went back to the house where her master was staying,
fell down at the door and lay there until daylight.—Judges 19:25-26

SHE

It starts with begging
through jagged breath,
dark night
      and the torches lit.
Shadows heaved
against the wall.
Jaw unhinged from the ramming fist,
I choke on heads, curses mixed with spit,
      Jehovah's disgust, flesh torn and bleeding
      from every thrust
while the moon bites its way across black clouds.
I lose track of hours, body count as
every orifice becomes an oracle:
"Let's see how this ends," voices chorus
and turn me over.
Screams silenced with grunts, my tongue
already turning to salt.

Lot's wife looks back on hell itself,
her mouth open in awe
and the last gasp at the breathtaking glow.

Stars fade, and the day calls
for all crimes to stop.
With one last plunge
they send me off to find my way home.
The slow, shivering crawl,
     naked, voice muted
dawn bringing only cold light
as my hands reach for a door
that will never open again.

WITNESS

It's the thunder as bones
rattle back into humanness,
        a crack of wings,
burning leaves, the tree forever scarred
by its own uncanny resurrection.

It takes faith in the battle
to highjack the moon, delay
the first hours of curfew
in the hopes that justice finds
her way back home.

It's the nature of intercession
to be driven by the fire's roar and spinning wheels,
        multi-eyed glory,
to be caught up in the rush of desert winds
speaking prophecies. *Come and see,*
it whispers, and you document
each image, each atrocity,
knowing at the end,
the dragon
waits for you.

FINDINGS

What man would love a woman
famine fed, with old gods
chasing her into strange houses?
I am Ruth, the widow who lusts
for milk and honey.

There is a time to go hunting among the reapers,
husking my hunger until I find
a table among the living,
a place where I can swaddle myself
in peaches and berries
until I grow sweet once more.

Then there is harvest:
the dying and gathering,
three men already swept up by the sickle,
and my every step haunted by Death.
Still you lay yourself down on the threshing floor,
eyes closed, waiting to see
who will reach you first.

SONG OF SAUL

The day you were anointed
I tasted oil in my mouth, felt
the slipping of kingdoms
from my hand, a slick move
to checkmate my time upon the throne.

If I could only find the right word,
the appropriate sacrifice to
ape my way back into grace,
you would sit at my feet, strumming
songs between the cracks of my sanity.

Instead, your face is always before me,
the frantic pulse and pursuit,
even as I hound after you, like hell,
harp strings wrapped around my tongue.
Muted words finally give way;
let me prophesy just once more:
it will be your star which rents its way
across my sky, a bitter and silent canvas.
But no matter princeling,
I die with your music in my ears.

*And there was a great famine in Samaria...and as the king of Israel
was passing by upon the wall, there cried a woman unto him,
saying, "Help, my lord oh king"...And the king said unto her,
"What ails thee"? And she answered, "This woman said unto me,
'Give thy son, that we may eat him today, and we will eat my son
tomorrow.' So we boiled my son, and did eat him: and she hath hid
her son."*—2 Kings 6:26-29

ON EATING A CHILD

Who would have thought the flesh
would satisfy both hunger
and taste? Malted   buttered,
we had to boil the meat
so the skin could simply
flake off with the touch of a fork;
we had already sold the knives,
had melted down the metal cups
and bartered away the silver, so
there was nothing else, really, to use.

And he had been so good
as I kissed him to bed that night,
his little head already drizzled in sweat
merely nodded and whispered *I love you*
as I walked out of his room,
into the kitchen where all the spices lay.

When he finally slept,
I crept in softly and pulled
the feather pillow over
his little rosebud mouth, gently,

like any good mother would.
His body, thin from famined
years, barely thrashed and
only slightly shuddered as
I hugged him close to a deeper sleep.

My friend's bony fingers
folded him into the pot
and we kept him unbroken, just like
Christ, believed in his sacrifice placed
on our tongues. In the midnight hour
we consumed this small blessing,
and with respectful silence, we ate,
our lips smacking with life.

DAVID AND JONATHAN

It was simple, really.
You spoke
and my heart fell,
a sack of grain
thrown to the floor,
scattered into wheatened pearls.

Everyone pointed to
the wreckage and gaped
in awe and wonder.

This, they cried, is love.

The Forgetting (Bathsheba's Lament)

My kisses don't relax the grim
corners of your mouth;
gone are the nights when we lay together
tangled and salted in moonlight.

That's the way
with age, to slowly
crack, split apart.

I half expected
my bed to be shaken out,
the sheets changed, locks
bolted. The nature of old love,
a bath long grown cold.

But still tell me:
this little one in your arms now,
with her dolly-skin
and hushed cherry lips,
with her legs wrapped
tightly around you,
does she bring you back
into the heat of battle?
In the dark winter months of your life,
does she warm you like the sun?

Who can find a virtuous woman? For her price is far above rubies.
–Proverbs 31:10

A VIRTUOUS WOMAN

I am the purple girl at market,
the crazy one with issues
of blood caking the underside. A sign
of stories to be told, my perfume
ready to be broken upon callused feet.

When I walk into circles, big as Grendel,
the timing is always wrong.
I am heavy with weeping to be done,
warriors to be eaten, leaning into empty tomb,
asking where the gardener is.

Despite all this, you can find me.
When dreams outhunt the wild caves
inside you, stick your heel
with poisoned arrows,
I'll throw poems into your eyes,
spit mud and water onto any wound
you please. We'll be healed the same hour,
legend has it, his word goes out.

THE PETITION (ESTHER'S TALE)

She didn't come to the party, so the story goes. Didn't twirl around for the heads of state or curtsy for the royal paparazzi. It was said the king's face grew red as a turnip and sent her off to one of the hidden chambers, never to be seen again. It's the law of social gravity: come when called, be invisible when expected.

The king sponsored the next beauty contest himself. No streamers to be worn saying what province we came from. Just a smattering of kisses and well-placed grunts as he tried each one of us on for the night. I was astonished that he remembered me in a sea of so many doe-eyed faces, yet I was no less flattered, for what little girl doesn't dream of being queen?

They don't tell you how to live with secrets. To be a forgotten people and still hunted.

Five years later, and I still don't know his middle name. It's been a month since we've had dinner, and the servants report he hasn't been eating well. Two nights ago my uncle scattered ashes into the air. *Go to him and beg him to reverse the irreversible,* he cried. Did my uncle not understand the nature of laws? Don't come unless called, die when appointed. They don't tell you how to stand between the living and the soon-to-be dead, petitioning for everyone to be saved. Whether it be from the sword or hell itself, it's no matter.

You come straight into the throne room of God with dirty sandals and all the appointments you didn't make yesterday, loaded with the cares of the world saddled on you like some sad pack horse. For three days and nights you stand and let them fall off one by one until your back unbends and you bring yourself upright and look Him in the face.

What is your wish?

When it comes your time, ask for every soul.

LEGION

I am the funny man
I am the sad man
I am the face
with a thousand voices.

My laughter fuels the sun,
hews the moon into teardrops.
This world, a stage where
the funny man jokes
and the mad man rages. Neither
can be chained in their delirious glory.

I am the naked man
with a grin as wide as the sky,
the haunted man with a tomb-dark heart.
The village priest tries to divine
my name; the country doctor
wants me to try the pink pill.
I take it, crawl out once more
onto the rocks, into the spotlight.
Below, the herds gather.

Mary(s)

I have crashed, moon-hungry, into the night,
clothes shattered, belly swollen,
skin punched hollow by starlight.

My husband looks on
from behind crib bars as I clump
into rooms full of stunned silence,
clicking tongues.
My brother dies, my sister tells me
it's time to do the dishes;
already, these mad sounds will not stop:
soft manger-rustle,
stones scraping together, the bang-clang
of hammer against nail,
the soft thump of nail against skin,
yet I push my way through voices,
hair gathered and ready,
only to find you scribbling in the sand,
rewriting the story.
The one they never get right.

SATURDAY

The stillness of the room explodes into our ears,
creeps into our blood.
Today, a riot:
The rumble of madmen outside
and torches ready for the burning.
Inside, we roar like bears, grope for the walls
like those blinded in death.
In this stone walled room
our madness whispers through cracks,
slips under barred doors.

Peter, crumpled in the corner,
croons himself to sleep with cock crows.
Your mother stands, cradles a small flour sack,
sings away in a manger as she rocks.
The other Mary doesn't move,
all her demons waiting at the edge of the gate,
calling her by the old names.

I lie still, eyes closed,
like one banished in exile,
son of thunder, beloved lunatic.
Thomas lies next to me, eyes wide and open,
never to shut them in blind faith again—
yesterday, we saw the sun nailed to the sky;
all our dreams are now rain.
Tomorrow will be nothing
but the gray ache of dawn.

GETHSEMANE

This fear   flesh-chained,
sweated beyond the taste of salt, blood dusted.
you feel the body like never before—
broken into pieces, four quarters,
a diced game where you are passed around
from one soldier to the next
before you're hanging from a tree,
naked as Adam
and just as dirty.

Even this garden holds shame;
the bent head, silent begging for cups to pass,
be filled with someone else's drinking.
Now you are the orphan, the sinner.
Your men huddle together, already widowed
    while angels flutter about like birds soon to die.
Above you, the barren hill,
broken skull, rusted nails.
A myth in the making, but always yours,
the dying.

HYPOCRITE

Because hate can mask itself as taste,
wishes to lick the spilt milk
of human kindness from every wound.

Because lust strips flesh off bone,
puppets its way into a child's room,
bouncing shadows
meant to be forgotten,
and casting stones sharpens the aim,
soothes the ear with moans
that mimic the ecstasy of love.

Because the gate is gold coated
and high as the tower of Babel,
the cries in the street barely a murmur,
crazy tongues prophesying:
a pretty ring for your finger
a millstone for your neck,
safe in the tomb where you
reign like a king.

MAGDALENE

I have often heard about phantom limbs
how they ache upon you
like some lost relative,
begging to have their cups washed,
another piece of toast.

The body remembers
when running was simple:
the minutia of each muscle contracting
against cold light, the art of forgetfulness.
No looking over one's shoulder, like Lot's wife,
to see the flames licking souls dry.

When I rammed my unholy frame
right into your feet, tears split down my eyes
and I felt the breaking,   cracked glass,   stained light,
blessed the new hollowed place
where you would be buried.

Wounds eventually draw themselves in;
I keep your memory swept up
the back of my neck, piled behind the mind.
Only when I walk forward
can I detect the slight limp
the unwanted halt, the forever leaning
against your shadow.

PAUL: AN UNPUBLISHED LETTER (FOR STEPHEN)

My lashes, suddenly full of angel dust,
crust into scales. Your face wraps
around my eyes, seals shut the lids,
traps the wrath of my justice underneath.
Chaos swirls into shadows, and I scurry about
like one of the three blind mice,
       arms lifted, fingers spread,
searching for a place in your dim outline
to hide me, to escape the inevitable,
the tail cut, my life maimed.
The butcher's wife keeps dancing,
stabs forward, fist curled, her hate
not being of the personal kind…
though she had to use that bloody knife,
knew it was meant for something grim.
       I blessed your lynch mob
when they came—hand raised, palm out,
go forth, go forth, see how they run.

Now, I am frozen in all this light.
The white cup shattered, my grave opens,
and for three days and nights
I swim in darkness, like Jonah—
mud and spit can only go so far.
Some visions want blindness,
need mind-madness to calm the killing logic.
Your head broke under the weight of our stones,
savage righteousness splitting spirit from soul;
and the King's men all waiting to gather your pieces.

Dreams scatter.
My sight slips back into focus,
but I will forever have this thorn in my side:
no matter what the grace or forgiveness—
I can never put you back together again.

A Virtuous Woman II
(Leah, Tamar, Rahab, Ruth, Bathsheba, & Mary)

We sheared our fairy tale dreams
walking the razor's edge
of marriage bed and harlot's veil,
deaf to the threats warning us to
  behave   behave
lest we be forgotten.

Shapeshifting, double dealing
with spies and kings, we lived
on both sides of the looking glass, bathed
in moonlight while keeping watch
for the star to be birthed from our stories.

But there were nights (weeks,
months, even) when we lay quiet,
still as death, straining our ear
for some kind of summons,
    waiting
for the order against our life,
the push into battle.
    That desperate waking.

Acknowledgments

I would like to thank the following people for all their help in looking at various stages of these poems. So many of them gave me insight, pushed me to say the unspeakable, find that priceless word, and so often, gave me the courage to keep writing. First thanks go to Valya Dudycz Lupescu, Ilana Teitelbaum, Melissa Root, Wendy Wagner, Kelly Cressio-Moeller, Jennifer Wagner, and Cynthia Kuhn for responding to all my late-night emails asking them to look at a few (or many lines) and seeing if they worked. A big thanks to Cynthia Reeser, editor of *Prick of the Spindle,* who took a poem I thought no one would publish because of its horrific subject matter; to Margo Lanagan and C.C. Finlay, who warned me when I was trying to pull my punches with imagery or a certain stanza; to Chila Woychik, for waiting patiently while I finished the rest of the book; to Anna O'Brien for providing the cover art and Francesca Myman, who designed the cover and also provided another set of editorial eyes; and lastly, to Rikki Ducornet, whose poetry class (which I took so long ago) pretty much changed my life.

CPSIA information can be obtained at www.ICGtesting.com
Printed in the USA
BVOW06s1825301015

424539BV00009B/62/P